Wakey! Wakey!

Lancashire Trips and Treats

Catherine Rothwell

Contents

ISBN I 872955 29 0

First published in 2003 by
Enigma Publishing, Huddersfield
Copyright © Catherine Rothwell 2003

Printed and bound in the UK by Dinefwr Press
www.dinefwrpress.com

Wakes Weeks

IF YOU ARE LANCASHIRE BORN and bred and nudging sixty years old you will surely have heard about Wakes Weeks rather than holiday weeks as they are now called. Maybe father, mother or grandmother worked at *t'mill* some time in their lives and well remembered that one glorious week of the year when the factory gates clanged shut. Spinners, weavers, slipper factory hands, felt operatives, tanners, machinists spear-headed a general exodus, because all the mills in the valley, glen or township closed down. What a quiet time it was for the stay-at-homes! Shops also closed, so those who could not join the mass evacuation had to stock up with food, bake or buy enough bread, meat, tinned goods and other groceries to last the week. Milk and eggs were obtainable because farmers could never go on holiday and in those days farms and dairies were still to be found amidst the community. My husband's Aunt Alice was perforce one of the stay-at-homes. Not only did she keep a cow in her orchard, which was milked daily; the hens also had to be fed.

After saving up in the Factory Holiday Club, the vast majority who looked forward to the event all year did go off at Wakes Week and in such thoroughgoing fashion that they left behind a ghost town - machinery silent, mill chimneys emitting no smoke. If, as the whole population devoutly hoped, the weather was fine, air grew clear and sweet. *Smog* went on holiday too. Suddenly, on a clear day, you could see for miles, the only bonus, besides peace and quiet, for those left behind. Where did they go? In almost all cases, to the nearest seaside resort, although a few were more venturesome, as we shall see. Sea air, sunshine, sea bathing, shrimps, oysters and basinfuls of fun were what hard-working folks craved for and, in so far as it was humanly possible, the proprietors of the resorts saw that they got it.

The Wakes! The Wakes!
The jocund Wakes
Olden times with garlands crowned
And rush carts green on every mound
Elijah Ridings

SALFORD WAKE

Will be held as usual on MONDAY and TUESDAY, the 30th and 31st August, 1819, with

EVERY AMUSEMENT

In the Old English Style.

MONDAY, a *Jack Ass Race* for a Purse of Gold, to be rode in true Jockey Style—no crossing nor jostling to be allowed.

N. B. There will be plenty of Bread and Cheese and strong Ale for those who bring Asses to Enter. No less than three to start except by permission of the Steward.

A Foot Race of a Mile for a good HAT, by Men of all Ages, 3 to start or no race.

LOTS of RIBBONS to be Danced for by *Old Maids* and *Young Men.*

A Young Pig will be turned out with its Ears and Tail Soaped or Greased, and the person who catches it first and holds it by either, will be declared entitled to it.

Grinning through a Horse Collar by Boys under 18; the best to have Five Shillings. 3 to start or no Race.

TUESDAY, *A Grand Smoking Match* by Gentlemen of all ages, for a Pound of Bagshaw's Tobacco.

Thick Porridge Eating by Boys under 18, the best to have five shillings—the second, three shillings—and the third one shilling—Six to start or no porridge.

A Sack Race for a good Hat—the second to have half a Gallon of Ale. Three to start or no race, without permission of the Steward.

A Good Hat to be run for by *Wooden Legged Men* of all ages. Three to start or no race.

A Grand Wheelbarrow Race, the best of heats for a Purse of Gold—the second best to be entitled to five shillings.

N. B. To prevent accidents, the Wheelbarrows will be inspected previous to the race by a person properly qualified.

If any disputes should occur, they will be decided by the Steward or whom he shall appoint.

W. CLAYTON, ESQ. STEWARD.

N. B. *The Amusements to commence precisely at Two o'clock each day.*

Wakey! Wakey!

LANCASHIRE OUTINGS one hundred years ago, give or take a few decades, often involved most of the village or township. Take Lytham as an example. After a dawn to small hours jubilation on the Club Day of 1894, 500 tradesmen and wives rose at 5 a.m. for a trip to Sherwood Forest and the Dukeries. Some must never have gone to bed but for the majority, to be up betimes meant the Town Crier or Bellman walking the streets clanging his bell. With no alarm clocks, no wireless and the weekday factory *knocker-up* off duty, this would be the best and only way of alerting the populace.

Handsome Kellerman Moore had the task in the Lytham of the early 1800s. These Jacks of all trades announced auctions, rewards, wreck sales, court cases, pig killings and in Poulton's early days the banns of marriage from the Market Square steps.

At Fleetwood in the mid 19th. century, steamers Cupid, James Dennistoun and Express, owned by Sir Peter Hesketh Fleetwood, besides making trips into the Bay, sailed up the coast to Piel Island, Barrow and Furness Abbey. Billy Whiteside's task, besides bill posting and crying the Fleetwood Chronicle in every street, was to ring his heavy *announcements* bell and get people up so that the boats could catch the early tide. Billy had a smaller bell for opening and closing the already famous Fleetwood Market, both bells being on view to this day in the Museum.

When outings were few and far between, every minute was precious. The first Sunday trips by rail, frowned upon by some as desecrating the Sabbath, made provision for *attending a place of worship*, so if you wanted to make the most of the day it was imperative to start early.

To this day, towns notably in the north of England have special holiday weeks to which they adhere, often corresponding in the calendar to the old wakes weeks, but the term is dying out. Will our children or grandchildren know what it means? How did the word originate? Before the meaning vanishes altogether it is worth looking into the mists of time. Wakes go a long way back in history, but the original practice has changed so much over the years it has become quite different from what was first intended.

Hidden away amongst warehouses and factories is the old parish church, which holds the answer, for wakes originated in an ancient custom that of gathering together on the evening before the birthday of a saint or the day appointed for the dedication of

THE

Cheapest & Most Direct

ROUTE TO

FURNESS ABBEY

AND THE

LAKES DISTRICT,

Via FLEETWOOD.

THE FINE  STEAMER

HELVELLYN,

OR OTHER SUITABLE VESSEL,

SAILS DAILY, (Sundays excepted,) BETWEEN

FLEETWOOD AND PIEL PIER,

IN CONNECTION WITH THE

LANCASHIRE AND YORKSHIRE AND THE
FURNESS RAILWAY COMPANIES.

*For particulars, see " Bradshaw's Guide," or small bills at all
the Stations.*

a church. The ritual was essentially religious, the night being passed in devotion and prayer.

The word *wake* literally means a vigil. Knights of old, before going into battle, setting off to the Crusades or engaging in tournaments, spent from sundown to sun-up on their knees before a church altar. Celtic tribes in early Britain practised wakes, important parts of death ceremonies when the mourners watched and feasted all night by the dead body, singing to protect the soul of the dead on on its way to the next world. To this end in Lancashire's Poulton-le-Fylde the custom of holding blazing hay on pitchforks continued into the 19th. century. The ancient name for the site of this ritual was Purgatory.

The *Knocker-up* in Bolton. Early 1900s

True wakes used to be held in England and are still observed in Ireland, when relatives sit all night by the coffin of the dead person. They eat, drink, sing, make music, ask riddles, weep and *keen*, play games, tell stories, in order to stay awake. Should they sleep in the house with the corpse, they may meet its spirit in dreams and themselves fall ill and die.

Although wakes in the north of England are connected with all-night vigils, they date from Saxon times. The missionaries in those days were anxious to replace heathen festivals with Christian ones.

Billy Whiteside, Bellman

Whenever a new church was built it was dedicated to a saint and thus that day became a holiday. However, before the feast it was stipulated that there must be fast. Each year, on the eve of the dedication day, there was to be an all-night vigil in the new church, but when the sun rose, watchers and everyone else in the parish set about feasting, dancing and generally rejoicing.

This custom of joy following the night of discipline survived all attempts of the Puritans to stamp it out. Dancing, singing, riding boxing, all manner of sports, even bear or bull-baiting, took place in the guise of a fair, usually on a Sunday, until at such places as Inglewhite where drunkenness and dissolute behaviour became so outrageous, it had to be stopped on the Sabbath.

During the Industrial Revolution even young children worked in mills from six in the morning until eight at night. No wonder they looked forward to the only week's holiday they could have in the whole year! Wakes weeks continued to retain their special glamour, from time to time even more allurement being added to them. There was also a gradual development e.g. the May Queen of old became the Rose Queen at the local Carnival. The commercial significance of individual mill towns featured, bringing on pretty girls as Cotton Queen, Silk Queen, Dairy Queen. Railway Queen.

So at different dates, and it is interesting to note that some do coincide with the Saint's day of the Parish Church, one town after another closed down and embarked en masse for the frolics and joys of a modern holiday. At the start of wakes weeks in the Lancashire cotton towns, all day long, charabancs and special excursion trains left for the country and the seaside. With sighs of relief, resplendent in *glad rags*, the operatives annually anticipated the time of their lives.

Programme of Events
Chorley Races 1815

Eccles Wake

Will be held on MONDAY, TUESDAY, WEDNESDAY, and THURSDAY, the 28th, 29th, 30th, and 31st of August, 1820.

On MONDAY, the ancient Sport of

BULL BAITING,

May be seen in all its various Evolutions.

Same Day,

A PONY RACE, for a Silver Cup.

Same Day,

A FOOT-RACE, for a Hat,

By Lads not exceeding Sixteen years of age.—Three to start, or no race.

On TUESDAY,

A JACK-ASS RACE,

For a PURSE of GOLD, value £50.—The best of three heats —Each to carry a feather.— The Racers to be shewn in the Bull-ring exactly at 12 o'clock, and to start at 2.—Nothing to be paid for entrance: but the bringer of each *Steed* to have good Dinner gratis, and a quart of strong Ale to *moisten his clay.*

Same Day,

A FOOT-RACE for a Hat,

By Lads that never won a Hat or Prize before Monday.—Three to start.

Same Day,

An APPLE DUMPLING Eating.

By Ladies and Gentlemen of all ages: The person who finishes the repast first, to have 5s.—the second, 2s.—and the third, 1s.

On WEDNESDAY,

A PONY RACE,

By Tits not exceeding 12 hands high, for a CUP, value £50.—The best of heats.—Three to start, or no race.

Same Day,

A WHEEL RACE.

Same Day,

A Race for a good Holland Smock,

By *Ladies* of all ages: the second-best to have a handsome Satin Riband. Three to start.

On THURSDAY,

A GAME AT PRISON-BARS.

Also,

A GRINNING MATCH through a Collar,

For a Piece of fat Bacon.———No *Crabs* to be used on the occasion.

Smoking Matches by Ladies and Gentlemen of all ages.

To conclude with a grand FIDDLING MATCH, by all the Fiddlers that attend the Wake, for a Purse of Silver.—There will be prizes for the second and third-best.—Tunes; "O where and O where does my little Boney dwell.—Britons strike home—Rule Britannia—God save the King."—May the King live for ever, huzza!

N.B. As TWO BULLS in great practice are purchased for diversion, the Public may rest assured of being well entertained. The hours of Baiting the Bull, will be precisely at 10 o'clock in the Morning for practice, and at 3 and 7 o'clock for a prize. The dog that does not run for practice is not to run for a prize.

The Bull-ring will be stamped and railed all round with Oak Trees, so that Ladies or Gentlemen may be accomodated with seeing, without the least danger.—Ordinaries, &c. as usual.

☞ The Bellman will go round a quarter of an hour before the time of Baiting. To enter for the Cups, &c. at the Duke of York.

GOD SAVE THE KING.

J. Patrick, Printer, Manchester.

JOHN MOSS, Esq. } Stewards.
T. SEDDON, Esq. }
T. CARRUTHERS, Clerk of the Course.

Penny A Mile

THE THOUGHTFUL RAILWAY COMPANIES issued leaflets cautioning punctuality, good behaviour, dress and safe keeping of railway tickets. *Glances on the Railway* pointed out places of interest en route for the new travellers, *Females Cheap Tickets* arranged from Preston by mill owners Horrocks and Swainson had to have railway staff on the alert for some men, trying to take advantage of the opportunity, masqueraded as women! During Summer, posters entitled *Sea Bathing for the Working Classes* were displayed in the mill towns. To the hard-pressed factory hands it was like manna from heaven. In the first month (July 1840) alone of the newly-opened Preston and Wyre Railway, 20,000 passengers were carried.

The lure to the country and seaside was irresistible: *To provide cheap railway travel for the more humble class of society, this Company commenced running their penny a mile trains from Wenesday last. What will our friends on the other side of the water think of this?*

The James Dennistoun Trading Steamer cost Sir Peter £1,226-18-10d., but to these *humbler classes* it would be worth its weight in gold. Travellers' tales filtered from coast and country to the sooty mill towns of Bolton, Manchester, Chorley, Wigan. Encouraged by these cheap trips, *folks were not backward in coming forward* as they say in Lancashire.

One man's description of a journey to Ardrossan opens with: *Left by an early train, the busy, noisy town of Manchester, right glad to escape the smoke and din of the factories and workshops.*

Besides sea bathing and sea water drinking there were also *rural sports* on a day out. The early bird could take part in a cricket match (*for a private purse*). There were pony, donkey, boat, foot, steeplechase, sack and wheelbarrow races, gingling matches and wrestling. Milk and buns were served from huge marquees, the sign being a balloon going up, followed by dancing on the lawn if weather permitted. What energy! This continued until half an hour before trains departed for home.

Richard Cobden paid for a mammoth trip which included a procession waving Free Trade banners. At Bamber Bridge, Bolton, Leyland, Rochdale, 1,300 jubilant workers assembled at 6 a.m. to join the specially chartered trains. Climbing to the top of Rivington Pike, Seat Naze, Holcombe Hill surmounted by Peel Tower and the nearby Grants Tower were favourite, up-at-dawn Easter attractions, when *pace-egging* or egg rolling was the chief sport, besides all that walking.

Richard Cobden and John Bright, successful industrialists campaigned in Parliament for Free Trade and the abolition of the Corn Laws.

The first iron barques in the port of Liverpool attracted crowds of sightseers as did Queen Victoria's first visit to her Duchy of Lancaster and on every such occasion early rising was the order of the day

Temperance Hotels sprang up to cater for the tee-totallers. John Livesey's instructions on Poor People's Trips were to: *buy tea, not to visit the beer shops. Persons intoxicated will not be allowed to return by the trains.*

It is noteworthy that the first accident on a home-bound train from the Lancashire coast was caused by a drunken passenger.

Tradesmen's Regattas open to all England included sailing, swimming, rowing, sculling events and some slapstick to raise laughs by *climbing the greasy mast*. Firework displays, balls, ploughing matches, archery displays, circuses, gas balloons, attended almost without exception by military bands, came later in the century, but it is obvious that one and all wanted these special days to last as long as possible.

Tired and sleepy, arriving back in their own towns, it was not uncommon to prolong the diesmirabilis with a procession around the streets, bringing to a close a host of memories which had commenced 18 hours before with the Bellman's Wakey! Wakey!

Waking

HISTORY SHOWS FEW DEMARCATIONS in customs, rather a merging of old with new, so that nobody can say exactly when the new took over. Watched over by a benevolent clergy, people surely retained those parts they liked best. Unfortunately, carried to extremes, some of the watches or wakes became so altered in character that instead of involving religious discipline with inoocent fun afterwards, they became opportunities for drunkenness and licentious behaviour which the clergy had to curb.

Before the official holiday week was established there were many single-day holidays throughout the year, some of which have survived as relics tangled up with actual Wakes Weeks and which vary according to the township. In spite of a 1536 Act of Convention decreeing that every parish should celebrate its wake on the first Sunday in October, this proved to be an Act honoured in the breach rather than the observance. Parishes who had celebrated annual wakes or feasts on their Church's Saint's day soon reverted to the ancient, favourite mediaeval habit.

So it was that staying awake in the local church the night before a holy day, i.e. the centuries-old custom of *Waking*, went on all the year round. However, by the time it had resolved itself into taking a whole week off work, the operatives hoped for fine, sunny weather and Wakes Weeks were held more generally in the summer months of July and August.

The Ferry to Knott End

Talbot Road in 1895 shows Rowley's Tobacco and Cigar Stores, patronised by visitors as was the Talbot Dining Rooms opposite the triangular area of land. Regular Wakes week holidaymakers would see this building, which opened for stage entertainment as the Arcade and Assembly Rooms, change to the Theatre Royal. It also served for a time as the town's Free Library and Reading Room. Sold again it underwent; further change in becoming Yates's Wine Lodge. Next to the Lane Ends Hotel, earlier visitors would recall Bank's Public Baths (Hot and Cold, Shower), to where sea water was carted from the shore.

Favourite Saints

PEOPLE HAD THEIR FAVOURITES in the Church's Calendar of Saints, perhaps feeling they could relate to some better than others, The feast of St. Oswald fell on August 5th, and attached to this was the Rush Bearing Ceremony. Until the 18th. century the beaten earth or flagged floors of churches were strewn with rushes to form a warm carpet and once a year these were cleared out and replaced. In the North of England and the Lake District this ceremony became linked with Wakes Weeks, Why not make a happy occasion out of a chore? The piled-high rush cart headed a procession and the mummers escorted it.

St. Swithin

Another popular saint was St. Swithin whose day falls on July 15th. The association with rain is derived from an ancient legend attached to the saint, who requested that he be buried outside Winchester Cathedral where he was Bishop, so that rain water would fall onto his grave. A hundred years after his death the local monks decided to move his tonb inside. On July 15th. it started to rain and went on for forty days and nights, The downpours and great storms were attributed to the saint's displeasure at having his wishes flouted and the *rain making* belief survived for centuries.

St. James

St. James's Day on July 25th. was popular as it heralded Midsummer, approaching harvest and the traditional time of country fairs. A pilgrimage to St. James's tomb in Spain was an alternative to the longer and more dangerous pilgrimage to the Holy Land. The sea special *wakers* each came back with a scallop shell, this being the saint's emblem. Several old grottoes remaining by the sea on the south coast and on the Isle of Wight were built entirely of shells to commemorate the St. James's Day Fairs.

Lammastide

The mingling of Celtic pagan practice with Christian ritual is well illustrated by Lammas-tide, the ancient holiday which eventually became August Bank Holiday. *Lamb Mass* was the time when tithe lambs were taken to the great tithe barns and presented, rather unwillingly, to the church. Some think it denoted the feast when bread for the holy Sacrament was made from the first corn of that year's harvest.

The exaction of titles by the Lord of the Manor, the Church and other land-owners meant that a tenth of produce (corn, hay, meat, honey, fruit etc) had to be handed over by farmers or peasants tenanting land. The commutation of tithes in 1836 abolished this method, which went back to Saxon times. They instituted a money payment instead.

Another connection is with Lugh, an important Celtic god, Lugnasand, harking back to the Dark Ages, was also a festival connected with harvest. Inspection of Celtic crosses in the Isle of Man for example shows a merging of Celtic and Christian symbolism. It was not surprising therefore that ancient Lammas customs persisted longer in the Celtic areas of Britain. Lammas tide in the Isle of Man was at one time an excuse for the wild behaviour and much drinking reminiscent of Bacchanalian orgies, This involved climbing Snaefell, but one clergyman was too smart for them. He was ready on the summit with a collecting box and an invitation to join in a church service. Ritual sacrifice to the old gods took place during the time of Lugnasand.

Lammastide is also derived from *loaf mass*. In Scotland it is counted a regular Quarter day and in England a half Quarter day. In Anglo-Saxon days *first fruits* were offered on August 1st, This was the first corn cut at harvest and in ancient days

Lancashire Rush Court. 1821

was offered to God. When offered to the Pope as, sums of money on the appointment of a bishop it was known as *annates*, a whole year's stipend.

St. Giles

On the feast of St. Giles dancing booths were set up and fiddlers brought in, One villager boasted that he had *danced his shoes right off his feet*. St, Giles is the patron saint of cripples, The story behind this is that whilst out hunting, Childeric, a King of France, accidentally wounded the holy hermit Giles, but Giles refused to be cured, remaining a cripple for life.

Churches dedicated to St. Giles were to be found on the outskirts of cities, some even outside the walls, as beggars and cripples were not allowed to pass within the city gates. One example is the famous Cripplegate, London, a church now completely enclosed by the concrete jungle of the Barbican Centre. The day for St. Giles was September 1st.

Were favourite saints connected with food? Trinity Wake Week fare included ham, plum pudding, stuffed bacon chine, wake-pudding and ginger beer. Wake pudding was made of bread and butter, eggs, milk, sugar, suet, currants and peel. In Cheshire frumenty[1] was the main Wake dish and at Westhoughton special pork pasties were baked and people came for miles on the baking day. Amongst the *sports*, many of them designed to raise a laugh, were: eating hasty pudding; smoking tobacco,' drinking very hot tea (at which the old ladies were best). There was a prize *for the first person to finish a plate of hot poridge and treacle eaten sitting on the church step*. The first man to get drunk at the Wake was dubbed *Mayor* for the day. The Rev. Hull in Poulton-le-Fylde, a market town with 15 inns, put a stop to this. Imagine what it was like in Preston in 1834 with a population of 50,000 and 190 inns. No wonder the Temperance Movement started in Preston, at the old Cockpit built by the Earl of Derby, where the population had *enjoyed the sport* of cock fighting as part of the Wake.

All Souls Day

All Souls Day, devoted to prayers for the faithful departed, is on November 2nd. According to tradition, a pilgrim returning from the Holy Land, stumbled upon a cleft in the rocks of an island. A hermit told him that the sounds he could hear from this cavern were the moans of the tormented in Purgatory. Odilo, Abbot of Cluny, hearing of this from the pilgrim, appointed November 2nd. as a day to be set apart in the Roman Catholic calendar to help all souls in limbo.

[1]*Frumenty. See recipe on page 35*

St. Margaret

St. Margaret was a virgin martyr of the 3rd. century, also known as *St. Marina,* The Greek Governor Olybrius wished her to marry him but she refused and was flung into a dungeon where she warded off a dragon by holding up the Cross, A young woman of great beauty and meekness, she is the patron saint of King's Lynn, an ancient borough. Her *day* was July 20th., although it is no longer upheld in the Roman Catholic Church. The feast day of *St. Margaret* of Scotland is November 16th.

St. Cuthbert

St. Cuthbert, a great Northern saint, was, like *St. Francis*, loved by all the animals. As a young man Cuthbert worked as a shepherd until one day he had a vision of angels coming to earth. Next day he heard that St. Aidan had died and he himself resolved to become a monk. Cuthbert spent many nights in vigil by the sea at Lindisfarne.

One Easter Sunday as *St. Oswald* and *St. Aidan* started their dinner, news came that many hungry people were outside. Oswald was then the King of Northumbria and he ordered that all the food be given to the hungry people and that the silver dish be broken up and the fragments also given to the starving. *St. Aidan* took the king's right hand and prayed that a hand that gave so freely should never perish. Like the body of *St. Cuthbert*, it was said to show no signs of decay for centuries.

St. George

St. George may have been an officer in the Roman army. It is unlikely that he ever fought a dragon but, associated with the Crusades and Agincourt, he was made patron saint of England by Edward III He features in the miracle and mystery plays, a favourite character for the mummers to portray.

St. Patrick

St. Patrick, the patron saint of Ireland, has many stories attached to him. He was a great traveller, converting people to Christianity and establishing many churches. He is said to have cleared Ireland of all vermin, down to the last wily serpent, and to have sailed across the Irish Sea on a millstone and landed in Lancashire at Heysham.

Odd Days Off

BEFORE THE ESTABLISHMENT of the full week's holiday for all, it is astonishing to discover just how many odd days were taken off work during the church's year. Collectively, they add up to far more than a week, so perhaps the mill owners were on a good thing when they so *generously* closed down the factories, for a solitary week.

An agreement drawn up on behalf of 200 apprentices in 1790 between Trustees of the Liverpool Bluecoat School and James Meredith granted 14 days' holiday at Christmas, Shrove *Tuesday,* Ash Wednesday and Saints' Days, an amazing six weeks' holiday a year, including November 11th. for Liverpool Fair and Guy Fawkes Night.

Most of the days fell on Saints' Days or to commemorate the Church's Year.

Gradually, the original meaning, strict ritual and the thinking process behind solitary and silent vigil vanished into the mists of time. The hold of clergy over populace weakened with the passage of years as social habits and laws governing them altered, when events moved out of the church and into the market place, but there is no doubt that some of our favourite festivals are older than Christianity and were once important days in the Celtic year. It is useful to remember that the old Roman calendar was based on 365¼ days in an average year. In 1582 Pope Gregory XIII deleted the ten extra days that had collected, but Britain did not fall in line until 1752 when we simply moved the date, changing September 3rd. to September 14th., thus losing those awkward eleven days and becoming like the rest of Europe. Old Christmas Day was on January 6th. The following are some outstanding festivals dating back centuries.

November 5th. which become *Guy Fawkes Day* was once *Samain* when the Celts lit bonfires to make sure that the sun returned after long Winter. *Samain* became *All Saints' Day*.

On November 30th., *St. Andrew's Day*, the slaughtering of livestock, particularly in the North of England, was carried out, the number kept depending on the amount of fodder available to maintain them throughout winter. Sheep were mated and the last of the crops cut, dried and threshed ready for storing.

Christmas and *New Year* were ushered in with much jollity and feasting. Eating and drinking kept out the cold, so the spiced ale wassail bowl was taken round to the houses of the village. All drank heartily, rewarding the cup bearers and wishing them prosperity An old carol was sung.

"Good dame at your door
Our wassail we begin.
We are all maidens poor.
We pray now, let us in
With our wassel .."

The old English word wassail means *be of good cheer* and elaborate wassail cups from Christmas and New Year feasting are much prized.

Mummers performed sword dances re-living the symbolism of death and the re-birth of Spring. This same group of mummers became the *soulcakers* in another season. On Twelfth Night the holiday was over. All the women on *St. Distaff's Day*, January 7th., returned to their spinning wheels and the men to the plough. The plough was blessed in church and agriculture resumed on *Plough Monday*, but still in holiday mood) later in the day young men fastened themselves to the plough and dragged it through the village, begging money. On that day new ploughboys were initiated before they could join the teams.

In some places the old way of celebrating Wakes with lots of good food and country sports was dying out by 1850. Watch night ceremonies on the Saint's Holy Day to whom the parish church was dedicated were in general still kept up as three days of jollity, until the end of the 18th. century. Added to a wide variety of activities were donkey races, jugglers, acrobats and mock elections as the electorate became more interested in reform of the franchise.

With the steady passage of time, during which conditions have changed radically, whole textile communities have died out. Although a relic remains in that the holiday list is still based on dates allocated to textile towns, Wakes traditions have also altered. Chorley, Leyland and Preston, once dead towns for seven days from the third Saturday in July, in 1952 introduced two holiday weeks overlapping with other textile towns. Overloaded Wakes Weeks had caused problems over travel and holiday accommodation.

A new generation was growing up, taking for granted holidays with pay. For our grandparents the Wakes dated from Saturday, a working day. Holiday Club money was all they had to spend, no wages being paid for the week off. On return it was a case of *tighten the belt till next pay day*, something dreaded by mothers with children to feed.

Blackpool, Morecambe, Southport, Isle of Man have had to give way to Costa del Sol, Cyprus and the Canaries, but old customs die hard, Doggedly, some towns retain their annual, time-honoured exodus even if not so widespread as before. With hi-jacking, terrorism and war, places like Blackpool are coming back into their own.

Building sand castles at Blackpool was easy with seven miles of golden sand washed twice daily by the Irish Sea but when tired of sands and castle-building there was that wonderful Blackpool Tower! Registered on 19th February 1891 the Blackpool Tower Company Ltd. saved £21,200 in its deal with the London-based Standard Contract and Debenture Corporation. Mayor John Bickerstaffe routed the London capitalists. By September the first stone of the Tower had been laid. A team of navvies dug out the foundations with picks and shovels. The celebratory banquet, attended by Sir Matthew White Ridley included haunch of Venison and Pudding à la Eiffel. Every bank holiday after opening, Blackpool Tower offered some new and entrancing addition to its visitors. The crowds came in their thousands to *Wonderful Blackpool, the most progressive resort under the flag.*

THE NEW
BOROUGH WAITS.

NOTICE:

The Public are respectfully informed that, I, Henry Dobson, late Leader of the Old Waits Band for several years, do hereby give notice, that, from the dissatisfaction it gave the public only hearing the Old Waits some twice or three times in a year, I have organised a New Band, knowing that one cannot give general satisfaction owing to the town being much larger.

The Old Waits have posted and distributed bills throughout the town calling us "Imposters," which is a base and false appellation; however, we will leave the public to judge of it for themselves; and, at the same time, beg to inform them that we shall not follow the example of the Old Town's Waits, viz., by carrying a book for the purpose of taking down the numbers of houses where they receive nothing, called by them "The Black Book."

Henry Dobson's Band will endeavour to the utmost of their ability, to please the Public, and hope that they will receive a share of their kindness and support. The Band comprises :--Henry Dobson, 1st Violin; William Widdop, 2nd Violin; Jonas Robinson, Piccolo; Abraham Wigglesworth, Violoncello; whom the Public will be able to identify by their Girdles, having on them " THE NEW BOROUGH WAITS."

Waits And Wakes

WHAT IS THE CONNECTION? A *wait* was the town watchman who cried the hours during darkness - *Twelve o'clock and all's well*, he would cry as he patrolled the streets, on the look-out for any wrongdoers such as burglars or grave robbers. He also had to keep a keen lookout against fire hazard. His duties passed on to the *Old Charlies* and the Bell Man or Town Crier.

The waits were the town musicians and singers who performed in the streets, especially at Christmas time when they became associated with the singing of carols, They did however perform and provide music on festive occasions throughout the year, so there is a connection with Wakes weeks.

Most towns had their Waits but in 1862 Bradford had a very special group - four blind men who fixed themselves to a pole and went round making music and calling at houses. Led by *Blind Sam Smith*, they had done this since 1829, but as the town increased in size the old Town Waits could not cover all the streets and Henry Dobson formed the New Borough Waits, who demonstrated one-upmanship by performing with two violins, piccolo and cello. The poster shows burning rivalry between the two groups.

Yorkshire especially became noted for its brass bands. Their beginnings were in the Church, Sunday School and Temperance Movement. Besides playing in the parks on public holidays they became much a part of religious parades and electioneering. Wealthy millowners financed and augmented these bands, many of which became famous and survive today e.g. Salt's Saltaire Brass Band, Black Dyke Mills Band and Besses o'th' Barn Band.

You must have music to invoke the holiday mood. Bands often accompanied the holiday crowds on board trains and pleasure boats. In its early years the North Euston Hotel at Fleetwood had a resident German band. The German street bands supplanted Waits bands.

In 1897 Clitheroe formed an Orpheus Glee Union which performed on many public occasions, including town holidays and civic events such as the Mayor's Dinner. The conductor was William R. Dugdale, the secretary T.A. Davies and in attendance was the whistler and mimic *Professor* Taylor, one of Clitheroe's characters. Supported by the nine members of the Orpheus Glee Union, he had a wide and varied programme. One great procession in Clitheroe was after William Garnett's presentation of a gold chain to be worn by the Mayor on all important occasions, The police, the town band, two halberd bearers, a mace bearer, three chief marshalls wearing white *ducks[1]* mounted on horses, plus Corporation officials, magistrates and javelin men paced the ancient streets.

Rochda Wakes, John Trafford Clegg's poem about Rochdale's annual holiday in 1890, describes hobby horses, quack doctors, pedlars, bogus *Professors*, a wild beast show, a circus, *Buckskin Billy and Indians*, brandy snaps, black puddings, hot peas *an' lots 0' things beside*. The Rush Cart, led by Morris Dancers, was a long-standing Rochdale tradition. Pageants were staged in some towns : Prestwich; Preston; Ashton-under-Lyne, Manchester and Liverpool.

A Free Spectacular - Felling a 270 feet high Chimney. This 1896 photograph shows the demolition of an unsafe chimney in Higher Broughton, Manchester The 270feet high octagonal stack was built with over a million bricks and weighed 4,000 tons. Mr. Joseph Smith, a Rochdale steeplejack, with five of his men, took only eight working days to cut away three parts of the base and insert 130 props. The props were covered with oil and other inflammable material and then burned away, thus causing the chimney to collapse bodily. When the bricks reached the ground they were practically undamaged. The operation was watched by a large crowd including many prominent engineers, whilst the factories were closed and most people out of town. When the rest of the community came home from holiday this was indeed a spectacle to boast about by the stay-at-homes. Lancashire steeplejack Mr. Fred Dibnah has used this time-honoured method, in his popular television programmes showing how, backed by colourful language!

When the chimney of Raby's brickworks was brought to earth by this method, Poulton Brass band played a loud accompaniment in 1911. Crowds turned up to watch.

[1]Ducks; clothing made of a heavy white fabric manufactured in Lancashire textile mills

Wakes And The Fairs

L AMMAS TIDE was the occasion for fairs. In his Wessex Novels Thomas Hardy makes reference to the great three-day sheep fair held at Trowbridge. St. Bartholomew's Day, August 24th., was the date of one of the most important, which was held at Smithfield for a period of 700 years until 1855. It had to be recognised as a great holiday and in the 15th. century it lasted for a fortnight. However, the trade emphasis had altered and it became regarded as the most important cloth fair in all England.

St. Bartholomew crops up in many places. In Cornwall he is the patron saint of bee keepers whose honey was widely used in the making of mead, witness the Blessing of the Mead by the monks near Mount's Bay. At a parish in Yorkshire where the church is dedicated to St. Bartholomew he was made into a straw effigy affectionately known as *Bartle* to be paraded around and finally stabbed and burned.

It is easy to see what a good time was had at the fairs with their sideshows, boxing matches, dancing, puppet shows, ribbons and laces stall, coconut shies, stilt walking, *fairings* for sale. It is also easy to see how a once solemn occasion finally devolved into becoming the annual holiday of a district. By 1791 a historian was writing:

The people of this neighbourhood are much attached to the celebration of wakes, and on the annual return of those festivals, the cousins assemble from all quarters, fill the church on Sundays and celebrate Monday with feasting with musick and with dancing. The spirit of old English hospitality is conspicuous among the farmers on those occasions but with the lower sort of people ... the return of the wake never fails to produce a week, at least, of idleness, intoxication and riot.

Outside the Station Hotel, Burnley, an advertisement in 1898 drew attention to *mantles and dresses*. The girls who went on holiday at Wakes Weeks in the 1890s could change their clogs and shawl for: a braided cap at 5/11d.; a lace blouse 1/-; a costume with ankle-length skirt costing 1 guinea and a pair of shoes for as little as 2/11d.

A hundred years before that it appears that men were more interested in bull-baiting *in all its primitive excellence*, At 11o' clock on the Monday in Eccles Wakes Week sports commenced, foot and donkey racing; but bear-baiting predominated. Fury, the bull, was centrepiece, the prizes being a fine dog chain and a horse collar. Bull-baiting was prevalent throughout the county as it tenderised the meat prior to slaughter.

Didsbury Wakes announced some gentler amusements in the Stockport Advertiser for August 8th., 9th. and 10th. 1825 such as a climbing the greasy pole; foot races; wheelbarrow races, prizes being *stuff hats*, panniers for donkeys, fustian trousers and pieces of pork.

The ancient Lancashire fairs on fixed dates were part of the Wakes tradition, many occurring in July, such as Lancaster, Garstang, Clitheroe, Oldham, Liverpool. Warrington's Fair lasted for ten days.

Compare these treats with *Stay at Home Holiday Attractions*. Burnley Fair Week July 1942 laid out in the official programme, price twopence: Colne Juvenile Follies; Mobile Cinema Van; Blackburn and Burnley Ballet Clubs; Folk Dancing; Sports and Gala and the Band of the East Lancashire Regiment playing at the Massey Music Pavilion, Townley Park. Burnley Agricultural Show, Burnley and District Canine Society were further events in wartime Wakes holidays. At an evening concert in 1943 Wilfred Pickles compered the programme whilst Rawitz and Landauer played, amongst other numbers, the then immensely popular Warsaw Concerto inspired by World War II.

What Did It Cost?

AS EARLY AS 1850 the cotton towns formed Clubs, levying weekly subscriptions to enable members to go away on holiday during Wakes Week. Chorley workers from Rice & Company were weekly paying members of Croft Mill Works Club, opened in 1850, Undoubtedly, the most important factor was the advent of the railway, *the great connector*, as a result of which many people could visit the Great Exhibition in London and racegoers travelled as far afield as Epsom for Derby and Oaks days, taking advantage of the midweek excursions which left Preston on Monday and returned on either Thursday or Saturday. For people who could not afford a full week's holiday, *departures in enclosed carriages* left Preston at 4.30 p.m. Saturday, end of June and returned Monday, beginning of July, most of these going to the Lake District.

Lancaster Road, Preston, around the turn of the century, was the home of Richard Stanley, an early travel agent who arranged mid-week trips during Wakes Weeks. He wrote to hotel proprietors, including Richard Rigg who inaugurated Rigg's Mail and Other Coaches as soon as the railway was brought to Windermere. Although Richard was reluctant to provide cheap accommodation, many in Blackpool, Southport and Lytham were willing to make arrangements for people just to stay overnight. Even this was too expensive for some. One Oldham man wrote: *After spending the day sight-seeing I got a night's lodging at a beer house for fourpence but, nearly spent up, I durst not ask for breakfast.*

One lady writing a postcard from the Pierhead Pavilion, Southport, informed her friend: *I have to pay one shilling extra to have a blanket under me. Two beds are five shillings.* In the 19th, century Blackpool hotel charges were: 5/- a day at Dickson's, The Royal and Lane Ends; Bonny's Hotel 4/6d. ; The Clifton Arms 3/6d. The Fylde Home Brewery had a price list for Wakes Weeks that sounds very modest now: *Ales and Stouts 2/6d. per dozen pints, Bass's Ale and Guinness's Stout 2/3d. per box,*

Southport summer holidays featured umbrellas to ward off the sun, bath chairs, elegant vintage pillar boxes and the longest seaside pier. There was a regular boat service connecting Southport with Preston and Lytham. One stunt in 1905 to attract Wakes crowds was Professor Osbourne diving from the Pierhead.

Southport in 1897. The pier, running nearly a mile out to sea, was one of the longest around the coasts of Britain and Wakes crowds enjoyed travelling its length by pier train, supplied in 1863. Called the Montpelier of the North, although the sea was retreating, paddling and boating were popular. In 1900 the tumult of the day ended in a firework display Professor Osbourne and Professor Powsey thrilled crowds by diving from a high board at the end of the pier. Large crowds came from Liverpool on the occasions of Queen Victoria's Diamond and Golden Jubilees. Southport's lifeboatmen were famous, especially William Bibby of whom it was said, He rescued 400 people from a watery grave. The wreck of the Mexico in 1886 was a national tragedy which cost the lives of two lifeboat crews.

Keswick. circa 1900

Wakes Trips And
The Temperance Movement

T HE RAILWAY COMPANIES offered attractive terms to private groups like Mechanics' Institutes and Temperance Societies. Thomas Cook, Baptist Minister and Temperance Man, like Joseph Livesey (the leading light in arranging trips to Fleetwood) persuaded Midland County to run special trains. Founder of the famous travel firm, Cook never looked back after this. In 1846 he arranged transport to Fleetwood and then on to Ardrossan by the steamer *Fireking*.

In recognition of the Temperance people, special tea rooms were set up at resorts and beauty spots, e.g. Jowitt's Temperance Hotel, Fleetwood, to cater for those who refused *strong drink*, At the Preston Cockpit in 1832 Joseph Livesey's voice rang out: *We will go with axes on our shoulders and plough up the great deep and the ship of Temperance shall sail gallantly over the land.*

The pledges of seven men were written in blacklead pencil on that occasion, but within a year the *Seven Men of Preston* had become 1,200 local people who, attending dinner at the Corn Exchange, had 1,200 gallons of water on the boil to wash down the meal. They were waited on by ex-drunkards!

Henry Anderton, Walton-le-Dale.
Temperance reformer 1809-1855

This contrasts sharply with Kirk Fair at Newchurch-in-Rossendale where for three days the streets were filled with surging masses of people who had walked long distances in summer searching for ale houses and arriving parched. At that time, the latter half of the 19th. century, ale was inferior although since Saxon times *ale conners* had seen to it that ale was *good, wholesome and of proper strength*. As with the greave or reed, their appointment had been annual. The last of the ale tasters in the Newchurch area was Richard Taylor of Bacup or *Spindle Dick* who taught a Bible Class every Sunday over his own beer shop. His ale was good, but when the appointment of ale-taster ceased, standards declined.

Just how far people did travel to the great fairs, usually on foot, is amazing. There is record of a man from Ashton – under- Lyne selling Lancashire frieze cloth at St. Bartholomew's Fair in 1553 at Smithfield, London where it was held for 750 years until 1855.

James Brooks   TODMORDEN

Sam and Emma Briggs, related to Sarah Fielding from Waterfoot. Rossendale Valley, 1890's

Guilds And Processions

ONCE A COMMON SIGHT in the villages of Lancashire, the ancient mumming plays devolved into pace-egging processions, The great attraction must have been that more of the villagers could participate. Wearing ribbons, laces, animal skins, the men and boys with their faces blackened, the maidens, *foregoing their wintry kirtle and lacing every bodice with bright green string* formed the procession. The traditional pace-egging songs rang out in the streets, eggs and money being collected on the route. Characters like Lady Gay, Soldier Brave and Old Tosspot the drunkard enlivened the scene.

It is easy to see how these jolly revels developed into carnivals, the processions getting longer as the years went by, with troupes of Morris dancers, more *characters*, tableaux and brass bands. Thornton-le Fylde in 1927 had a procession, one mile long, with 1500 children taking part.

In much the same way Club Days, which originally consisted of men-only processions carrying the silk banners of their Lodges or Friendly Societies, developed into Galas and Festivals, drawing in the ladies, girls and children. Decorated floats expressing various contemporary or humorous themes began to appear and inevitably a pretty girl was crowned queen amidst her retinue of page boys, courtiers and maids of honour, a throwback from the May Day ceremonies of old.

As interest grew, more time and money was spent. Competition between schools and churches became fiercer, the annual queen being chosen in strict rotation from one or other of the sects. A century ago Lytham's Club Day was considered the high spot of the year. Octogenarians Misses Livesey and Fenswick recall sitting up all night to make paper roses to decorate the wrought-iron arch at Castle Gardens, Carleton for Gala Day.

Ancient Guild Processions like those of Preston and Longridge had their connection with the 14th. century city craft guilds later known as Livery Companies which acted as trade organisations for fixing wages and standards of craftsmanship. On special occasions their members wore a distinctive costume or *livery* and numbered amongst them were Mercers (founded 1393), Grocers (1345), Drapers (1364), Fishmongers (1448), Salters (1558), Vintners (1436), Clothworkers (1528). There were also Apothecaries, Butchers, Blacksmiths, Glovers, Farmers, Plasterers etc., some so rich and powerful they founded schools such as Merchant Taylors' or Goldsmiths' College. So much money was lavished on a Kendal Guild one year that it impoverished the town and the processions were suspended.

Perhaps the most famous is that of Preston which holds a Guild only once in twenty years and whose fame draws people from all over the world. The celebrations go on for months culminating in grand processions through the streets involving the Mayor, Corporation and Civic regalia.

Many townships like to include tableaux or pageantry directly connected with authentic, historical incidents in which their ancestors took part. Enacting such scenes as the Vikings sailing up river and landing to found settlements or skirmishes from the Civil War complete with cannon supplied nowadays by The Sealed Knot is stirring stuff and ever more popular.

Originally, the period immediately preceding Lent, ending on Shrove Tuesday, was Carnival time, the word being based on the Latin meaning *a farewell to flesh*, signifying no meat eating during the Church's season of Lent. Gala Days meant festive days when people put on their best attire.

Preston Guild. 1922

Wakes Recipes

MY ANCESTOR, great-great-grandfather Edward Hoghton made Braggat Ale at the Dog Inn, Belthorn. His parents haled originally from Yate and Pickup Bank, a tiny hamlet near Haslingden, where no doubt this ale was drunk on other occasions besides Mothering Sunday. Although no precise recipe is available, I know that he added honey and ginger to the mulled ale. My father, born in Belthorn, later of Blackburn, always referred to Mothering Sunday as Fig Pie Sunday. Mother's recipe was.

Make a good shortcrust pastry with 8 ozs lard and 16 ozs flour. Rub well in till the mixture resembles bread crumbs. Made with lard the pastry can be rolled out thinly, which is the pre-requisite of a good fig pie.

The dried figs were soaked in hot water and sugar, cut into long strips to fill the pie dish generously. I remember it as a gorgeous fruity pie to be indulged in before redcurrants, damsons, bilberries and raspberries became available again.

Ollives were considered part of festival fare. These consisted of thin slices of veal stuffed with sage, mention being made of them as far back as the 1600s. Beef olives are presumably in direct descent. Over-eating at the Wakes and Festivals sent people to consult old Herbals:

Customs Watch House, Fleetwood.
Wakes Cakes taken up the River Wyre on boat trips from here. 1890

He needeth neither physician nor churgeon that hath Self Heal and Sasnicle by him, wrote Parkinson in 1640, whilst Gerard at the same time was advocating, Put caraway seeds amongst baked fruits and cakes to help digest wind.

On Pancake Tuesday, as a girl at Waterfoot, mother remembered singing *Pancake Tuesday is a very nice day. If you don't give us holiday we'll all run away.* (For authentic pancake, caraway and simnel cake recipes *see Catherine Rothwell's Lancashire Cook Book. 1999*)

Gingerbreads were so popular at fairs throughout the land that they became known as fairings.

Ormskirk Gingerbread

10 oz flour	*1 lb treacle*
4 oz cinnamon	*½ oz ground ginger*
12 oz butter	*1 lb sugar*
¼ oz mace	*a little grated lemon rind*

Melt butter and mix with treacle and sugar, Add flour, lemon, cinnamon, mace and ginger. Beat mixture well. Drop very thinly on a well greased tin and bake in a moderate oven. Cut into squares   Curl each round your finger. Keep in a tin.

Eccles Cakes

¼ lb flaky pastry	*½ oz candied peel*
2 oz currants	*½ oz melted margarine*
1 oz granulated sugar	*nutmeg*

Mix margarine, currants, chopped peel, sugar and nutmeg. Roll out pastry thinly and cut into rounds. Place mixture on each. Damp edges of pastry and gather together. Pat into rounds. Snip each top gently with scissors. Brush with water and sprinkle with sugar. Bake in a hot oven for 20 minutes.

Lancashire Wakes Cakes

8 oz plain flour	*5 oz sugar*
1 oz currants	*4 oz butter*
1 large, free range egg	*milk to mix*

Rub fat into flour. Stir in sugar and currants. Mix to a stiff dough with beaten egg and milk. Knead until smooth and roll out dough to 1/8th. inch thick, cutting into rounds. Place on greased baking sheet and cook in a moderate oven for 15 minutes or until golden brown. Cool on wire tray, dredging generously with sparkling sugar.

Frumenty

Frumenty was basically *creeded wheat*. My grandmother referred to a good rice pudding as *nicely creeded*, meaning that it was not sloppy, the moisture being adequately absorbed.

After hulling the wheat was put in an earthenware bowl and covered with water, to be placed in fire oven and left overnight to simmer gently. The following was added next day.

2 pints milk
4 oz currants
grated nutmeg

4 oz raisins
4 oz brown sugar

To be cooked gently on hob for another hour at least.

An *extraordinary large Twelfth Cake* was cut in 1811. Twelfth Cake was customary on Old Christmas Day but can be traced back even further to the Roman Saturnalia. Members of the household drew lots to determine the King, a personage later corresponding to the Lord of Misrule when a bean and a pea were inserted in the large plum cake and whoever found them were King and Queen respectively until midnight. The ceremony of cutting the Twelfth *Cake* was one of the last of the Christmas season. The *extraordinary large* cake, 18 feet in circumference, weighing nearly half a ton and containing amongst other ingredients 1,000 eggs, was made by Adams of 41, Cheapside, London. Portions were packed off to all parts of the United Kingdom, including Lancashire.

Soul Cakes And Tosset Cakes

Soul cakes made from oatmeal and aromatic seeds were eaten on All Souls Day. Goosnargh still specialises in them. The inkeeper's wife at the Bushell's Arms used a grater a yard long for her cone of sugar in the 1900s.

Carling Sunday in Lent was when steeped peas were fried in butter and eaten during the afternoon. Cinder tea was made for the new-born baby to sip, the red-hot coal dropped in water signifying warding off the Devil.

Extraordinary Large

Twelfth Cake,

18 FEET IN CIRCUMFERENCE,

TO BE SEEN AT

ADAMS's, 41, Cheapside,

OPPOSITE WOOD STREET.

———————————

This Cake considerably surpasses in size any that has hitherto been made in London, or, in fact, in the world: its weight is nearly Half a Ton, and actually contains Two Hundred and a Half weight of Currants, and upwards of ONE THOUSAND EGGS.

This Wonderful Cake is ready for Public inspection, as above, where orders for any part will be received, and duly attended to.

N.B. Cake packed for any part of the United Kingdom.

Jan. 3, 1811.

These and many other customs preceded Wakes Weeks and in a long transitional period became part and parcel of them.

New inventions and sophistication stealing into the lives of factory girls and boys killed off most of these customs. Perhaps the greatest survivor is the chocolate Easter Egg, modern version of the pasque or paste egg, symbol of fertility and new life.

At the weekend after August 12th. in the Lancashire village of Stalmine people ate Tosset Cakes on Tosset Sunday. St. Oswald's was the old name for St. James's Church, Stalmine. Tosset was Oswald's nickname.

The eating of Soul Cakes, especially in Crookdale Lane, which led to the great Moss of Stalmine and Rawcliffe, signified that for every cake eaten, one soul was freed from Purgatory, a prayer being said as you ate. It was a time to remember the dead. Candles were kept burning on graves and tombs. Soul Mass became Saumas, another kind of spiced, sweetened cake. One Lancashire woman preserved a soul mass cake in her family for a century. It was believed to bring good luck.

This 92 year-old photograph shows the men's bathing area at Port Skillion, Isle of Man, with one of the steamers from Liverpool in the background. Besides Port Skillion, where gentlemen were charged threepence to use the dressing rooms and stone platforms, there was another popular bathing place near Douglas called Port Jack at the northern end of the Bay. Bathing machines and boats at Ramsey, *Queen of the North*, were kept for the visitors on the south shore. Even in 1877 catering for the influx of visitors was the town's greatest activity from Whitsuntide to early October. That year the number was estimated at 150,000.

The Improvement Commissioners of Fleetwood numbered about 20 and their job was to implement the Fleetwood Improvement Act passed by Parliament. These gentlemen in their tall *chimney pot* hats were responsible for arranging the visit of Queen Victoria in 1847. They included Dr Ramsay who was the town's chief officer for Health, Robert Banton who built and occupied the first Inn on Dock Street, Joseph Bisset, T. Walmsley, R. Seed and R. Porter. The engine *Fleetwood* made the first journey along the Preston and Wyre railway line when it was opened in 1840. In later years it was put to use in making the Docks but there was so little money to spare that at one meeting of the Commissioners they decided not to light the few street lamps when there was a full moon.

A Royal Wakey, Wakey

*W*E ANCHORED AT SEVEN IN FLEETWOOD HARBOUR. *The entrance was extremely narrow and difficult. When I went on deck there was a great commotion, much running and calling and pulling of ropes. It was a cheerless evening, blowing hard..... At 10 o'clock we landed and proceded by rail to London.*

Queen Victoria wrote this in her diary in 1847. It was the first visit to Lancashire of a reigning monarch since the days of Charles II. The royal yacht Victoria and Albert had sailed rough seas from the Isle of Man following their customary holiday at Balmoral in Scotland. Victoria, a friend of Sir Peter Hesketh Fleetwood, founder of "the newest town in all her dominions" wished to call on 20th September, 1847.

The loyal subjects were in panic. Notice was short and so was cash. Building had nearly bankrupted Peter, but Mr Yates, from Manchester was hastily summoned to carpet a saloon with scarlet cloth and drapes. A throne was knocked up. J W Sharp, head boy of Rossall School was also knocked up. He was a roused from sleep to start work on royal address of welcome. In Latin!

But the weather was conspiring to do its worst. The Town Commissioners confidently announced that provision would be made for 50,000 spectators to see the approach of the Royal Squadron and the landing. Next day it was hence to the royal carriages and the royal train.

At 6 o'clock on Sunday evening the Royal Squadron was expected, 20th September and her Majesty would stay on board all night, to debark on Monday morning when she would proceed to London by train.

What of her loyal subjects! To see their famous Queen and her family with all the trappings of a royal reception - well this had to be a the trip of a lifetime. They rolled up in their thousands. Special trains were laid on from Todmorden, Halifax, Manchester, Bolton, Liverpool, Blackpool and Preston. The Preston and Wyre line, opened 1840 was geared to carry 6000 passengers alone. From break of day, rowing boats plied across the River Wyre carrying the rustics from Preesall, Knot End, Pilling, Hackensall and as far away as Lancaster.

But the weather! At 11 o'clock the wind was blowing so hard and the rain falling in such torrents that the four steamers scheduled to be welcoming party dare not leave port.

During the day, a Guard of honour arrived from Manchester and the royal train steamed into Fleetwood from London Euston (extra track had had to be laid, but the impecunious commissioners had seen to it). This raised hopes but high-water came and went. The sodden crowds realised it was not to be on that day. Disappointed but undaunted they trailed back to the special trains and their homes. There was still tomorrow! In true Lancashire fashion they came back next day in their thousands.

Monday dawned stormy, wild and cloudy. high-water came and went but still they waited, eyes strained seawards. Would she never come?

At 6 o'clock the signal gun boomed, fired by Mr. Porter and the official party made for the scarlet saloon at the Pier Head. The Squadron approached, Undine and Fairy escorting. Mr. Gerrard, experienced Fleetwood pilot was aboard the royal yacht, fortunately so, for such was the strength of the illumination from the North Euston Hotel and Pier the gas supply failed. The lower Lighthouse refused to function.

As the yacht turned gracefully around Steep Breast at precisely 7.15 pm the patient crowds burst out cheering, suddenly the scene turned to pure enchantment. The Moon sailed from behind clouds, rain ceased and the royal family assembled in the glass rotunda on deck were visible to all. For the rest of the evening, a display of fireworks was kept up to amuse the royal children, but the Queen had to be left undisturbed.

Next morning, it was Albert, Prince Consort who was up very early, climbing the Mount to view the town, in building. It was a beautifully clear morning with nobody about.

Special trains brought in even greater numbers of trippers and at 10 o'clock Her Majesty set foot for the first time on her Duchy of Lancaster.

After her long Balmoral holiday she looked brown and fit. She smiled, waved and walked firmly but slowly with her family to the royal train. What did she wear?

A white satin bonnet hung with white feathers, a yellowish orange shawl and lilac tartan dress. Once they overcame their awe, the impression of the crowds was of a small, dumpy figure in excellent health and spirits.

With Sir John Hawkshaw in charge of the train, off chugged the Royals to London and the crowds, yet again, went to their special trains. The Queen had given them indelible memories of a unique trip, generally agreed to be a bobby dazzler by Lancashire and Yorkshire alike.

To Sir Peter Hesketh Fleetwood, Victoria gave the white kid gloves she was wearing and the quill pen with which she had signed her name in the red saloon. These tangible mementoes are carefully preserved to this day at Meols Hall, Southport.

Easter Tide To Christmas

T HE 40 DAYS OF LENT may well have once been an enforced fasting period when supplies of food were running out. The ancient merry making of Shrove Tuesday before the fast began was a last fling.

During Lent a holiday was always allowed for all maids and apprentices to visit their mothers, carrying a bunch of violets or a simnel cake. Bury grew famed for its simnel cakes and for its braggat, a spiced ale drink on Simnel Sunday or Mothering Sunday. Out came that favourite country dish frumenty again followed by fig pudding or fig pie.

Well into the 19th. century Easter Day was marked by *lifting*, which commemorated the rising from the tomb. On Easter Monday the women were lifted into the air by the men and on Easter Tuesday the process was reversed. Some of the inns had special chairs covered with satin and decked with ribbons for favoured guests to sit in and be *heaved.* Christopher Sansom wrote *It was a boisterous day. What merry scenes! What humour in the faces of these Lancashire witches!*

Even the local squire was approached with, *If you please, sir, it's Easter Tuesday and we've come to lift you.* It shows that something of the meaning of the church festival was retained but it was translated into holiday fun and *how holy days became holidays* might best describe it.

At Eastertide Lancashire village children, e.g. at Weeton, carried baskets lined with moss and filled with small cakes and eggs. Pace egging, the rolling of eggs, as at Avenham Park. Preston, expresses the rolling away of the stone from the sepulchre of the crucified Christ.

The Jolly Boys or pace eggers were welcomed by Beatrix Potter at her home Hill Top in North Lancashire. It was believed that when the sun rose on Easter Morning it danced with joy at the Resurrection of Jesus Christ.

Our ancestors also regarded the first cuckoo call as very important. Should a farmer hear it whilst standing on grass he was assured of a bumper crop of hay. Some people still write letters to The Times about it!

On the first of May the chief *May Day* festivity was when oxen drew the Maypole to the Village Green. Draped with garlands of flowers and ribbons, it was followed by joyous bands of people who danced around it. Even the oxen's horns were garlanded with flowers as the Lord and Lady or King and Queen of the May were elected to preside over the festivities. Morris dancers followed with bells fastened to arms and elbows, their tinkling to warn off evil spirits. Winter had passed and they had survived its rigours and dangers, so high spirits prevailed whilst the availability of freshly grown foods once more gave them vigour.

Behaviour on May Day in Hyde Park, 1654 was denounced in the Modern Intelligencer: *Much sin was committed by wicked meetings with Fiddlers, Drunkenness, Ribaldry and the like,* but *Maying* was generally considered great fun. In high spirits whole parties went off to the woods to bring home boughs of hawthorn blossom. The damage done led to landowners putting out the story, *If you take hawthorn into the house your mother will die.* May was the month when witches got busy. Birch and rowan were spread over thresholds to keep evil spirits at bay.

In May Day games, Jack in the Green or the Green Man, the Hobby Horse and the Fool moved amongst the dancers. Inn signs denote old festivals and customs. As The Bear was popular, so was the Green Man.

Even today great-grandmothers can remember May 29th. as Royal Oak Day or Oak Apple Day which joyfully kept up the restoration of the Monarchy. You rose early to get oak sprigs to wear in your lapel. Anyone not sporting the oak was chased and *nettled* bare legs lashed with stinging nettles.

Perhaps the final manifestation of the old village wake lies in the Whitsun Walks or Club Days when Friendly Societies processed with banners. These last in areas of the Fylde for example devolved into Galas and Festivals: Poulton-le-Fylde; Singleton; Bispham; St. Michael's-on-Wyre; Lytham.

For centuries *Whitsuntide* (White Sunday), the seventh Sunday after Easter, was celebrated first as a pagan festival then as an important part of a Christian feast. The 1871 Bank Holiday Act marked Whitsuntide, a famous Wakes week, as a national holiday, the beginning of true Summer and moment of exodus for thousands of mill workers to go to the seaside.

The traditional Sunday School walks or field days commenced during this great week when almost everybody bought new clothes and shoes. In Garstang, the ancient market town, it was known as *Wissenda.* Friends and relatives from the countryside flocked into the town. Photographs showing little girls in white dresses date from the

1900s when a field day was held after the procession in the big meadow behind the parish church. Baskets covered with white cloths held stacks of sandwiches and fruit, to be given out to the multitude. The day finished with foot races and rural sports for all ages. At night there was dancing that went on until the small hours.

On *Midsummer Day* dry, midsummer wood was burned whilst dancers circled sun-wise and as the flames died down cattle were driven through the dying embers to protect them throughout the year. The singeing of foals and calves was an ancient ritual.

On Midsummer's Eve some parishioners spent the night in the church porch, hoping to see the souls of all those who would die in the village during the following year. Although frowned upon by the clergy, the custom persisted.

In Lancashire, Longridge Fell, Rooley Moor, Rivington Pike and Seat Nase were lit up by midsummer fires. On old Midsummer's Eve, July 5th., before the change of the calendar in 1752, a custom called Barning the Thorn took place and still does at Appleton, Cheshire. The ancient thorn tree in the village is dressed with ribbons and garlands whilst villagers dance round it.

Beating the bounds took place when the elders of the township led the young men and boys around the boundaries to impress upon them the land rights of a community. The passion for land and the retaining of it by families was as strongly felt by the French peasantry as by the English. Emile Zola's powerful novel *Earth* leaves no doubt. In France also the keeping of Wakes was a solemn duty.

Much and many were the fun and games attached to *Harvest Home* suppers after the gathering in of the crops. Everybody had helped, from young children to old ladies. In bygone days this was the most important social and economic event of the year, for a good harvest was something to rejoice over. When the reapers had cut the last sheaf of corn it was the custom to raise it into the air and give the Harvest Shout:

Well ploughed, well sowed,
Well harrowed, well mowed.
And all carted to the barn
With nary a load throwed.
Hooray!

A corn dolly, symbolic of the Harvest Spirit, was made on the spot and kept on a shelf until Plough Monday. August 1st. marked the beginning of harvesting and

September 29th., Michaelmas, the end of harvesting. Because it was now possible to assess the yield of fodder and the number of animals that could be kept, Michaelmas heralded a time of great fairs and animal sales. Garstang was one Lancashire town famed as far away as London for its horse fairs.

Christmas absorbed many pagan festivals, Yule logs and candles being associated with the Norse. Although Prince Albert introduced the custom to Britain in 1841, long before that the candle-lit tree was thought to shelter woodland spirits when the trees lost their leaves in winter. Old Roman Saturnalia customs ended on December 25th. They were still observed in the Middle Ages when a servant was crowned Lord of Misrule to preside over ceremonies which commenced with the dragging of the Yule log into the Great Hall. Boar's head was the main dish for the Norse, to be replaced as the years rolled by with goose, beef and turkey. In Lancashire *letting in Christmas* was as important as *first footings* on St. Stephen's Day when at midnight a dark stranger entered the house, holding a sprig of green. January 20th. was the *Eve of St.Agnes*, the 30th. the feast of St. Basil.

Wagonettes setting off in 1902 for the day's tour of *Windmill Land* as the Fylde of Lancashire was then known. The cobbled square of the mediaeval market town of Poulton le Fylde, with its stocks, cross, fish nab and whipping post, attracted even Charles Dickens. The large carved bull under the inn sign was strong enough for landlord Mr. Croft to sit astride on Gala days when it was decorated with coloured ribbons and flags.

Trips And Treats

NINETEENTH CENTURY BLACKPOOL certainly *packed them in*. The following quotation explains how this was done. A single house, not large, frequently receives 120 people to sleep in a night, 5 or 6 beds are crammed into each room and 5 or 6 people into each bed ... but, they cannot be stowed at one time. Those who have the places first are roused when they have slept through half the night to make way for another load, and thus everyone gets his night's rest.

The Metropole was built on the site of Bailey's Hotel (dating from the late 18th. century). Bonny's was known as *Old Margery's*.

A Blackpool directory of 1867 reports 13 bathing machine proprietors, 27 hotels and inns, 240 lodging houses, one temperance hall and six beer houses. Shops, elegant news and coffee rooms had even been built. Because of the rising importance of the town, there was some anxiety among the residents to *render the sojourn of their visitors pleasant and comfortable*.

The thatched cottage with wooden partitions and an open ladder to the loft was another type of accommodation to be found at Marton or Poulton-le Fylde, for all visitors could not be put up in the town itself.

By this time, 20,000 excursionists were leaving Manchester in the summer, notably in August when factories were closed, including Isidor Frankenburg's, which had become the Greengate Rubber and Leather Works. During the Franco-Prussian War his operatives manufactured waterproof army knapsacks, (originally he had started in 1867 with 12 hands). The work forces of H.J. Glaister & Co., cotton manufacturers and the Adelphi Brewery swelled numbers in July.

This account goes on to explain that for months the colliers' wives and families have saved every available penny and for these annual excursions whole towns are deserted, excursion trains packed to suffocation. They spent the savings and came home penniless, *leaving hundreds of pounds behind at Blackpool or other seaside towns.* In 1900 Lancashire miners were paid five shillings a week but the cabinet portrait of one young Eccles miner shows how smart they could be, Lewis's 30/- suits were advertised on the sides of Blackpool Pier.

During Wakes Weeks when the mills were closed some factory owners arranged free mid-week excursions for their workers, one of the first being in 1846 when Richard Cobden, the proprietor of Crosse Hall Calico Printing Works, Chorley, gave a day's wages to his operatives and laid on a trip to Fleetwood. The photograph shows the main street of Chorley where on return the workers processed with two

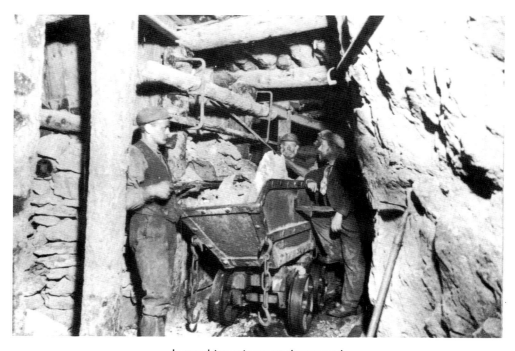

Lancashire miners underground

The 1880s photograph of Market Street, Chorley shows a thatched cottage on the left. This ancient thoroughfare would once be lined with them and has been the scene of many processions including the Whitsuntide arrays from St. George's Sunday School, The churches' *last Saturday in June* parades in Chorley were true forerunners of Wakes Weeks.

brass bands as they had done in Fleetwood. *The festivities were not ended until the night was far spent.* This indicates what a great occasion it was.

Of all the workers of Lancashire the colliers are the most sociable. Unlike the weavers, the spinners, the ironworkers and those employed in the 101 trades of Lancashire who go off for a whole week's holiday at the Wakes, the colliers prefer to go now and then for a day's excursion to the seaside but they all go together.

The early *wakers* were also walkers, some actually coming on foot all the way from Manchester. According to Moses Heap, cotton spinner from Rawtenstall, a few carts made the journey in 1813, carrying *old ladies who were rheumaticky, going on a jaunt to the seaside.* The Manchester pilgrims brought tea and sugar with them, paying ninepence a day for lodgings at the seaside. From Padiham groups known as *Padjammers* travelled in carts with provisions for a week and stone jars of fresh water slung between wheels. They returned with sea water to drink at home, calling it *physick*. Whilst at the seaside, bathing in the sea and drinking lots of sea water.were the order of the day.

Poulton Market Place: Cross, Stocks and Whipping Post circa 1850. Trippers loved to be photographed with their legs in the stocks. Early postcards show black-bearded James Danson, local character in the Stocks. James was born in 1852 and lived in Potts Alley, just off Market Place.

Some trippers journeyed in wagons, riding in turns and used their vehicles to visit neighbouring towns during their stay. *The great green meadow* was what they called the sea and it was enjoyed to the full, used for drinking, bathing and sailing. All these carts and wagons were later replaced by coaches but it still took time. The Quicksilver Coach running from London to Devon took 21½ hours to cover 219 miles at a speed of around 10 miles an hour. Twenty minutes was allowed for travellers to take breakfast and there were 23 changes of horses.

The immense number who came to Blackpool in August made 1827 a remarkable year. Carts and other conveyances brought visitors from Preston, Blackburn, Burnley, Colne and Yorkshire mill towns, many willing to sleep in outhouses and barns, although some complained. This occasioned one old lady to say, *What will the world come to? People were once content to be twelve in a bed but now they are constantly grumbling if they sleep with five.*

Parties of neighbours joined up in what was called *a round robin*, hiring the loft area under thatch or slate where sixteen or so could lie down (four in the one bed - taken in turns during the night). Others slept in the coaches which later ran from Preston to Lytham and Blackpool on a regular basis.

The sleepers in barns and outhouses were welcome for meals at the farmhouse provided they paid a small sum. As late as the 1900s a sevenpenny tea could still be had in the Yorkshire Dales. Here is a description by John Sharland of how they fed in 1850.

We dined off pewter plates, a great display of which with dishes decorated the dresser. Our meal consisted of boiled salt beef and boiled pork together with two or three kinds of vegetables all cooked together in one large crock hung in a crook over the kitchen fire. We dined at the long deal table and the farm labourer, a boy and a servant girl all sat with us at the bottom with a very coarse cloth to eat off. Each partook of a basin of broth from the crock with coarse bread broken into it.

In August 1827 vast numbers of carts rolled up from Blackburn, Burnley and Colne. People slept in barns and stables, many having to find lodgings in Poulton. There was a rhyming couplet about Blackpool's accommodation going back to 1790.

Old Ned and old Nanny at Fumbler's Hill (later the site of Carleton Terrace)
Will board you and lodge you e'en just as you will.

Winter Gardens
BLACKPOOL.

General Manager · Mr. JNO. R. HUDDLESTONE.

UNRIVALLED ATTRACTIONS. Daily until further notice.

GRAND
Variety Entertainments

All Day, and every day, from 11-0 a.m. to 11-0 p.m.

MAMMOTH PROGRAMME THE GREATEST AND GRANDEST IN BLACKPOOL.

GRAND PAVILION at 2-0 and 7-0, First Production of the Entirely New and Novel
SPECTACULAR BALLET, entitled—FROM

MONTE CARLO TO JAPAN

By Mr. JOHN TILLER's Famous Company of over **100 ARTISTES!** Special Scenery and Effects, representing

Scene I The Terrace and Gardens of the Casino, Monte Carlo.
Scene II.—The Deck of the Wonderful Air Ship, "The Cloud Climber." Scene III.—A Street in Tokio, Japan.

Grand Ballet of Japanese Flowers and Fete of Lanterns.

In the VICTORIA ANNEXE, INDIAN LOUNGE, and CAFES, at intervals during the day, from 11-30 a.m. to 11-0 p.m.
First Appearance in England this Season, direct from Italy, of the Favourite

DELLA ROSA BAND NAPOLITAN SINGERS AND DANCERS,

Who made such an Extraordinary Success Last Season.

The Grand Empress Ballroom and Indian Lounge
The most SUMPTUOUS and PALATIAL HALL in the World will be open for

DANCING

EVERY AFTERNOON AND EVENING AT 2-0 and 7-0.

This Ballroom is acknowledged to be the Most Spacious and Most Beautiful in the World.
The Luxurious Indian Lounge, Ornamental Gardens, and Promenades.

A VERITABLE FAIRYLAND! ALL ON THE GROUND FLOOR.
BRILLIANT ILLUMINATIONS!!
Grand Orchestra. Conductor: Mr. J. H. GREENHALGH.

ITALIAN GARDENS. Running Daily from 11 a.m. to dusk (Weather permitting)
THE NEW AND NOVEL SENSATION
LES MONTAGNES RUSSES

From the MOULIN ROUGE, PARIS, AND THE PARIS EXHIBITION.

A Delightful, Healthy, and Invigorating Trip, travelling through the Air at a speed of twenty miles an hour.
A Ride in the Cars - 3d. each per journey.

PING-PONG ALL DAY IN THE GRAND CAFE.
Special Regulation Tournament Table.

Refreshment Buffets and Grand Billiard Room
Chops and Steaks from the Silver Grill. Celebrated 1s. Teas.
Grand CAFE AND RESTAURANT, Coronation Street.
Luncheons, Dinners and Teas at Reasonable Prices. CHOPS and STEAKS from the Silver Grill.

Ubangi Savages, The Golden Mile, Blackpool. Princess Ubangi a pygmy from a central Africa weighed 42 lbs and was insured for £10,000 *A perfect specimen of the human species*. Besides appearing on the Golden Mile she attracted large crowds in Toyland at R.H.O. Hills Ltd. Store, Oldham Street, Manchester. She was 28 years of age and 30 inches tall.

Dr. W.H. Cocker Blackpool's first Mayor 1870

Early Wakes weeks visitors could thank Dr. W.H. Cocker, Blackpool's first Mayor and great personality, for their entertainment.

As a Director of both the *Winter Gardens* and the *Prince of Wales* Theatre, he gave the *Winter Gardens* a spectacular send off by inviting the Lord Mayor of London to perform the opening ceremony and accommodated him and other dignitaries at the *Imperial Hotel* at his own expense. In its early years the *Prince of Wales* was a financial disaster, as was Dr. Cocker's private venture in opening an aquarium, menagerie and aviary on the Tower site in 1877, which six years later he had to dispose of along with other property. Subsequently, the London-based Standard Debenture Corporation acquired the site and suggested forming a company to build the Tower. Thanks to the shrewdness of Alderman John Bickerstaffe, who by then was the Mayor, the Londoners were thwarted in their hopes of making a quick killing and the Tower Company was North-West owned.

From a magical distillation of sun, sea air and entertainment Blackpool evolved to become the playground of Lancashire, to where the majority of northeners flocked

A very old photograph showing ladies in crinolines c 1860 on a trip to Furness Abbey. They sailed from Fleetwood at 6 a.m. on the James Dennistoun or the Cupid. Early tourists could buy a Penny Guide to Furness Abbey, and the hotel of that name was *one of the ideal hotels of the United Kingdom*. Weekend terms in the early 1900s, from dinner on Saturday to breakfast on Monday morning, all inclusive, was 1 guinea. The lady second from the left is thought to be Fanny Jameson born at Parrox Hall, Preesall, and the wife of Captain May Jameson, Civil Engineer to Sir Peter Hesketh Fleetwood, founder of the town of that name.

The Great Wheel, Blackpool Winter Gardens.

in Wakes Weeks. This original programme from 1902 gives some idea of the crowded, luxury theatre they had dreamed of visiting.

Press reports in 1885 prove the Manchester businessman Mr. W. H. Broadhead had taken over the *Prince of Wales* Baths, where he showed fabulous water displays to the holidaymakers, Professor Finney, champion swimmer of the world, being the first performer. By 1896 impatient shareholders were clamouring for its redevelopment as the Alhambra, which was eventually sold to the Blackpool Tower Company Ltd. It *is* a fact that. on the evidence of his doctor, William Broadhead moved to Blackpooi for the good of his health.

The Lancashire coast gained much praise from early Wakes Weeks travellers in 1832 when the cholera epidemic never touched it although visitors came from

Blackpool Sands 1870

inland towns where hundreds were dying from the terrible disease. Such healthiness was praised by those who took refuge in Blackpool and in October a special service of thanksgiving was held, the sermon being preached by the Rev. Cummings.

Blackpool Sands was a great gathering ground for all types of showmen. As a very small girl, I can recall one man hurling sticks of pink rock into the crowd. C. J. Toole (if your hair is falling out a few applications will stop it) could command an audience of hundreds.

Standing in front of his huge banner emblazoned *Toole Hair King* and flanked by big drums, he claimed : *This remedy is made from a recipe belonging to Queen Catherine of Hungary... If you are bald, it will make the hair grow again.* It was claimed that Ino, sprayed in the face, removed scurvy, blackheads and pimples. *To mothers it is a boon to cleanse their children's heads from nits and parasites* There was even an analyst's report from Stonyhurst College backing all claims!

Dancing on Morecambe Pier was always popular as was the free roof garden at the end, and of course inshore sailing and fishing. When Richard Ayton called in the early 19th. century at this tiny fishing village once known as Poulton-le-Sands he was amazed to find *visitors from Lancaster, Bolton, Preston and other industrial towns, come for the benefit of the physick in the sea.* Passing Blackpool, he saw *legions, full of motion, continually splashing in and out of the water.*

DONKEYS ON THE SANDS, MORECAMBE. No 464.

This is the Morecambe of 1918 when shrimp fishing in *nobbies* was carried on in the Bay and a steam ship took *Wakers* to Grange-over-Sands when the tide was right. The donkeys were busy, their bells jingling merrily as they trotted up and down the beach. It was always nice to see them arriving in a herd each morning with the donkey drover and to pat their noses and read their names on the strip of harness just below their ears: Bessie; Rosey; Mary, We were told they spent the winters in farmers' fields having a rest and that some lucky children, if their father had a stable, were allowed to keep one of the patient animals during that season. If the *whiffler* in the Morris Dances whipped away winter illnesses and bad fortune, as he was supposed to do, Morecambe's *sea* breezes and mountain air from the Lake District did more.

Central Promenade
Morecambe.

Blackburn Market

The cost of travelling by slow, heavy, stage wagon then averaged a penny a mile, but coach travel was expensive e.g. from Halifax to Blackpool was 18/6d. By the end of the century the Lancashire & Yorkshire Railway even advertised in French *Visit the pleasant beaches of Blackpool, Southport, Morecambe and the Isle of Man.* Everywhere the piers were the central attraction of the resorts.

Hopwood and Sons of Blackburn, who employed 1,200 people in 1848, hired a band to accompany their work force to Blackpool. Some people could not afford to buy food so the benevolent Hopwoods had prepared for this contingency. *Two hundred loaves and three hundredweight of Lancashire cheese was stowed in a horse box to provide refreshments.* This was reported by the Blackburn Standard, whose offices were situated not far from Blackburn Market where this busy scene was photographed 100 years ago.

About this time the most popular seaside resort was becoming so crowded that the Railway Company allowed people to sleep in the carriages. Even with this facility, *a great number had to walk the beach all night*, reported the Preston Chronicle.

As railway lines extended, trips into Yorkshire and Wales became popular. In the mid-19th. century many wanted to see Menai Suspension Bridge and by the 1930s it was possible to sail from Liverpool, Princes Pier to Anglesey on the St. Tudno and St. Sieriol. Chester and Beaumaris, old places with castles, attracted visitors as did Furness Abbey. *The Abbeys of Old England*, which included Furness, was a series of penny guides designed especially for tourists by Edward J. Burrow.

Lancashire party setting off from Rhyl, 1912. This group, which includes Jessie Howarth of Cheetham Hill, Manchester, seated next to the man holding the baby, is about to set off from the White Rose Booking Office, Rhyl, for a charabanc tour of Snowdonia.

Photographed by Mr, Lord of Poulton, this girl at Enfield Mill, Wigan with two gaffers to keep an eye on her looks happy enough to be contemplating an early Wakes week. Mill lasses wore black stockings and clogs, fents, and belts for reed hooks and comb, used on the weaving looms. Kem Mill at Whittle-le-Woods, Cuerden Mill, Withy Trees Mill, Stone Mill, Orr's Mill in School Lane, Aspden's and the Bamber Bridge Spinning Company (referred to as Wesley Street New Mill because it was the last mill to be built) all closed down at Preston Holiday week.

At Grange-over-Sands which appealed, as did Lytham, to those visitors wanting a quieter, more genteel resort, tourists could have their photographs taken seated under a large umbrella, with a painted back-drop of the Lakeland mountains and Morecambe Bay. This wonderful period picture shows the graceful dresses of 1900 and the old-fashioned tripod and camera under a black cloth. Behind the photographer, *licensed to take likenesses*, would be his portable dark-room with all the chemicals necessary to develop the heavy, whole-plate, glass negatives.

Bands accompanying excursion trips during Wakes weeks appeared indispensable in the 19th, century. This one from Bowness played on the Lakes steamers. John Robinson of the Steam Yacht Company at Windermere offered trips on the lake for holiday parties throughout the Spring and Summer seasons. Another enterprising Bowness man, James Haddart, had gardens and nurseries *well stocked with a choice selection of plants, flowering shrubs, fruit and forest trees*. Facilities for pleasure and picnic parties amidst his *small collection of*

birds and quadrupeds drew Preston and Lancaster people. The third class fare from Preston to Lancaster was 1/8d., from Lancaster to Kendal 1/9d.

Lytham Volunteer Band.
2nd East Lancashire Regiment,
outside Lytham Hall.

Those who preferred peace and quiet after the bustle of crowded trains in Wakes weeks often went to the Lancashire resort of Lytham where there were *pleasure, strawberry and tea gardens*, sedate donkeys on the beach and a quieter pier, but in the earlier years, no decent bathing machines, newsroom or carriages to take people to church on Sundays in wet weather. Indeed, in a number of resorts bathing machines were used as conveyances for this purpose. Lytham later amalgamated with the fashionable St. Annes-on-Sea. The Ladies Orchestra at Lytham St. Anne's flourished for years, *declared the best concert on the Fylde Coast.*

Although Scarborough in the 18th. century allowed bathing in the nude, when the craze for immersion and imbibing of sea water struck the country, many resorts

St. Annes Pier Orchestra, 1937

were restrictive. Off the coast of Devon was a bay so suitable that *a thousand men could bathe there with no difficulty.*

Rules at Blackpool involved the ringing of a bell which warned the men to withdraw so that the ladies could change *and sport themselves amongst the waves like a colony of mermaids*, as William Hutton put it in 1788. He it was who said of Blackpool : *The tables are well supplied ... shrimps are plentiful, six people make it their business to catch them at low water. The place yields only one spring. The fresh water is carried half a mile but I thought it the most pleasant I have ever tasted.*

Avenham Park, Preston, remains the time-honoured place for rolling Easter or pasque (paste eggs), one of the old customs kept up for years before the traditional Wakes Weeks emerged. This postcard sent by Cissie in 1904 (*one more for your collection*) is also interesting for the Tram Bridge and Avenham Tower.

Rowson, in his *Curiosities of Lancashire*, much read by tourists, wrote ; *Many years ago a horse-drawn railway used to carry goods between the Lancaster Canal Terminus in Preston and the Summit between Brindle and Bamber Bridge. Known as the Tram Road, it passed under Fishergate by a tunnel and over the Ribble on a bridge which still exists and then across Avenham Park,* All good Wakes country!

Avenham Park, Preston

Paddle steamer *Waverley* in 1977 when she last visited the Lancashire coast and carried holidaymakers. She is the oldest paddle steamer still in service, having been launched in 1946, and has undergone a refit of £350,000 under the direction of the Paddle Steamer Preservation Society.

Foudroyant Lord Nelson's flagship wrecked off North Pier, Blackpool, 1898. Mr. G. Wheatley Cobb of Caldicott Castle had restored and refitted the *Foudroyant* as a show ship to attract Wakes Weeks crowds. It cost him £20,000. After a short spell at Southport, *Foudroyant* came to Blackpool but on 16th June, 1897 a freak summer storm dragged the heavy oak ship from her moorings and shattered her so badly that *huge old timbers were ripped in every direction, every internal fitting and bulkhead swept away and the decks rent to pieces.* Even more trippers from all over Lancashire and beyond poured in to view the wreck and collect souvenirs such as copper nails. Walking sticks, boxes, tables and other furniture were later made from the oak and the ship's copper was transformed into bowls and commemorative medallions. An ill wind for *Foudroyant* but not for Blackpool.

Another crowd puller was the barque *Clara* wrecked in December, 1906 on her way from Norway to Preston, a trip she had made without mishap on 24 previous occasions. The 430 ton wooden barque was built on 1857 at Miramichi and was captained by Olaf Petersen. Carrying 56 tons of wooden deals she had tried without success to obtain a pilot a mile south of Nelson Buoy. At midnight in a heavy squall her keel struck bottom. Continual bumping caused the rudder to break and main topmast to crash down I carrying away sails. The crew took to the ship's boat seeing that capsize was imminent but they were blown helplessly over the treacherous sandbanks until landed by the Fleetwood lifeboat at 8 a.m.

The lifeboat signal gun brought hundreds on to the Promenade to watch the drama unfolding and , although it was winter, subsequent weeks saw extra trains running on the old Preston and Wyre Railway route, bringing in the sightseers.

Captain Jack Ronan who in his career, commanded every vessel in the Isle of Man Steam Packet Company's fleet and carried thousands of passengers to the Isle of Man from Fleetwood and Liverpool, still keeps up links with the Fylde coast. Gaining his Mate's certificate in 1957 he became Chief Officer under Captain Lyndhurst Callow, master of the Lady of Mann which was purpose built for the flourishing Fleetwood trade Jack has been photographed with hundreds of *Wakers* particularly on *Ben My Chree* and *Snaefell*.

From the Windsor Woollies' factory in Poulton le Fylde, staff came to southern seaside resorts to entertain holiday crowds. The girls who produced the beautiful knitted woollen suits and bathing costumes actually modelled the clothes they made for adults and children. Much was the delight when Queen Elizabeth (now the Queen Mother) and George VI accepted kilts and jumpers for the two princesses Elizabeth and Margaret Rose. There were many Lancashire people in this crowd who came to Southend with them in the summer of 1930

Norbreck
Swimming Baths

Jim Rowlands, in spats, top hat and frock coat, stands outside the ancient Parish Church of St. Chad, Poulton-le-Fylde, beside his vintage bicycle fitted with a horn. The occasion was the Victorian Market Weekend of June 20th. 1992. This mediaeval market town, like many others, is endeavouring to revive its long history in a number of ways, not least being its annual Gala.

At the end of Wakes Week, arriving and departing in the early 1900s, the excursion platforms at Blackpool were appropriately filled with trains bound for the mill towns. in those days Burnley, Padiham, Nelson, Preston, Colne, Oldham, etc., all had their own particular week. For North East Lancashire it now commences on the first Saturday in July.

From Southport Chapel Street Station with its *direct route to Liverpool, Manchester, Leeds, Bradford, Halifax*, people assembled for the trek back home. By sea from Douglas the Isle of Man Steam Packet Company ship, Viking, a legend in its day, returned to Fleetwood with a full complement of passengers at the end of their holiday. Many amusing stories were told about people who boarded the wrong trains.

As soon as they got back to the grind, most workers commenced saving for next year. Having something to look forward to was the spice of life which made drudgery bearable. Lancashire's wry sense of humour is shown in a popular song from the turn of the century, referring to one young man fresh from a Wakes Week and *back to fifteen bob a week.*

> *Who should bring his plate of hash in,*
> *But the girl that he'd been mashing*
> *By the sad sea waves.*